Lead
Follow
and
Succeed

The Tango Way

C. A. Soto Aguirre

Lead
Follow
and
Succeed

The Tango Way

C. A. Soto Aguirre

𝑘

Kavyata® Publishing

Ann Arbor, Michigan, USA

k

Kavyata® Publishing

P.O. Box 7270, Ann Arbor, Michigan 48107, USA

www.kavyata.com

Book design and cover photography © by Kavyata® Publishing.

ISBN-10: 0-9749391-4-5

ISBN-13: 978-0-9749391-4-8

Library of Congress Control Number: 2010910058

First Edition

Kavyata® Publishing is a division of Kavyata® Group, LLC.

Ann Arbor, Michigan, United States of America

Chapters

To all of you who wish to lead,
                but don't know how to follow.

To all of you who wish to follow,
                but don't know how to lead.

To all of you who wish to succeed,
                but don't know the way.

And to all of you who have found
                the tango way.

C.A.S.A.
Ann Arbor
Fall 2010

Lead

Follow

and

Succeed

The Tango Way

The Lead

"Everybody please stand up, hold your chest high, pick your chin up, and be confident. If you aren't confident, you'll find it difficult to lead and succeed in tango or in life."

That was the first thing the tango instructor said to his new group of tango students. They were ten: five women and five men. Each of them burdened with their own issues and aspirations for life, coworkers at a venture capital firm in New York City. The instructor, Carlos, was an Argentine fellow widowed ten years prior. He and his wife first met the day she took a tango lesson in Buenos Aires, and since that day, for forty years, they were dancing partners. She had died of pancreatic cancer at the age of sixty. His career as a dancing instructor had kept him in good physical shape and it was hard to guess he was seventy-five, especially because every weekend he routinely dyed his hair, eyebrows, and mustache jet black.

The first lesson for his ten new students was about to start. It was the middle of the Summer and the air conditioning had been malfunctioning for days. They were standing in a small room in the 101th floor of a skyscraper in New York City, with a magnificent view of the Hudson River weaving though the city and the city's busy night lights. The room was one floor above the headquarters of Paxoramic Capital, the firm they all worked for. John M. Crawford, the young CEO of PaxCap, had sent this group of promising financial leaders to Carlos' tango boot camp, but hadn't told them why or under what criterion they were chosen to participate. They believed it had been a blind-folded selection, but it wasn't.

The students were a very diverse group of people, as is common in New York. Wilmer, Raymond, Augusto, Jerome, and C.Y. were the men; Natalia, Virginia, Miranda, Kashi, and Camila, the women. The room was too small for eleven, but according to Carlos it was better so, because he wanted to bring intimacy to his students. The floor was a beautiful light brown maple wood and the high ceiling lent a feeling of roominess to the place. Carlos had asked to have one wall covered by a full-wall mirror, and there was also a big balcony that allowed them to go out for a cigarette if they wanted to. Virginia and Jerome were the only smokers in the group.

Carlos asked his students to talk a little about themselves, so that he could memorize their names more easily. Camila, the most attractive of all women in the room, raised her hand and said,

"Before we introduce ourselves, I want to know why we are here. Who decided that we should take this class?"

Carlos smiled to her and replied. "Your boss John M. Crawford and I met fourteen years ago, while he was visiting his grandfather in Buenos Aires. This may be a surprise for you, but yes, he has Argentine blood running through his veins. I decided to call him by his middle name, Manuel, which he inherited from his grandfather, Luis Manuel Ripetti. Luis was a very good friend of mine and a beautiful tango dancer as well, a true *tanguero*. Manuel took my private tango lessons when he was in your position. He now believes that those lessons transformed him into the CEO he is, at such a young age. I am sure he is not much more than forty years old. Soon after Manuel was named CEO he called me to set up this class with a group of financial advisors, and here you are. You should be happy that you are among the "chosen" because that means Manuel believes that you have the potential to replace him."

Camila was a petite slender African American woman with big sparkling eyes, curves that resembled a violin, and was just twenty-three years old. She smiled back for two reasons; she liked the idea of becoming the CEO, but also, she felt attracted to this old guy who talked with so much authority and confidence. Age was not an issue for her as she was dating a guy twenty-eight years her senior already. That was a clue to her character: conservative, looking for protection, not a risk taker.

"I dream being the CEO! I am Camila and I joined the company one year ago after graduating with honors from business school. I am confident that the knowledge I got in school will serve me for the rest of my life."

She was too young to know better. Life is a constant change, and no single set of rules or firm knowledge can serve one for an entire life. Next in line was Raymond. He was using his phone to send text messages, while everybody else was paying attention to the class. Camila elbowed him and he realized it was his turn. With very masculine manners he closed his cell phone and said,

"I am Raymond. I came to New York from California three years ago. I enjoy chatting on the Internet, reading, kayaking, running, cycling, photography, rock climbing, music, and playing chess."

He liked spending time at gay bars, something nobody would imagine by looking at him, having such masculine grave voice that resonated in the room as if he had a megaphone. He had always been involved in many activities, which had hindered him from advancing faster in his career. Lack of focus is terrible. Focus is the art of finding inside you the deepest talent to overcome the challenges you are confronting, and that takes concentration in fewer and fewer things. Raymond was still living with his mom, and had never had a girlfriend.

Carlos smiled, knowing he would have to work a bit harder with Raymond to help him focus on his tango learning. He knew well that life presents itself with many options, but the goal is to be happy, allowing and helping others to reach their own happiness as well. With that single premise he lived his life without distracting his thoughts in religion, politics, or any other issue. Tango was Carlos' channel to achieve happiness.

Augusto was standing next to Miranda, on whom he had a crush. He had been trying for months to ask her out on a date, but haven't built up the courage to take action. He had always been held back by not taking the first step. He was hoping that some day Miranda realized he liked her and that she would take the initiative, but that hadn't happened. He inherited his

short height, tanned skin, black hair and a war-
rior gaze from his Mexican ancestors who had
immigrated to Texas three generations ago.

"My name is Augusto and I've been working
with this company for five years."

And he went quiet. People were waiting for a
longer introduction, but he turned his head to
Miranda, waiting for her to talk.

"Okay, I am Miranda. I can tell you one more
thing about Augusto. He is a quiet guy, as you
already guessed, but he is very talented at his
work. He brings more customers to the company that all of us combined. So, don't get
fooled by his lack of words."

That comment was very gratifying for Augusto.
He never knew she was so aware of his achieve-
ments. A big smile blossomed on his face, one
that he hid from Miranda, but that everybody
else noticed.

"Well, about me," continued Miranda, "I came from Spain when I was 3 years old, and have lived in New York ever since. I love going out for dinner, waking up late on weekends, and taking my dresses to the dry cleaner."

She had just given away her main fault. She didn't like to take on long tasks. She was lazy and impatient to such degree that eating out and using the dry cleaner were indispensable to her life style. Even her long brown hair was taken care of weekly by her hair stylist.

Next in line was Wilmer, a forty-year-old hard working guy, not very tall and a bit chubby. He had the kind of glasses that made him appear to have big eyes, framed in black. Quite the opposite of Miranda, he preferred to work hard to achieve his goals, but he had a big problem. He had never been very innovative or creative. His motto was "work hard and get the reward." He had created a routine in his work that made him look like a stubborn and narrow minded person. One major concern in his life that no-body in the room knew was that his daughter, Carol, had been born with Down syndrome fif-teen years ago.

"I am Wilmer. I was born New York, but my parents are from Germany. I always liked danc-ing, but didn't have time to try it because of my long working hours. This is a great coin-cidence. I mean, my job now includes dancing; that's awesome!"

Next to Wilmer was Jerome, a handsome black guy from Alabama. He dressed sharp, with an expensive caramel color suit and fine leather shoes. He was tall and muscular, a playboy from all sides, but he couldn't hide the stench of his cigarettes.

"I am next. I was named after my father, Jerome, who taught me that fifty percent of success comes in the form of appearance. If you present yourself well, you are half-way to your goals."

That was a pitiful introduction. Jerome hadn't been a successful financial advisor for years. In fact, he was a man without dreams or goals, and had wandered through life showing off his physical beauty and taking advantage of it. He was in trouble, because the new CEO had given him this last chance to demonstrate his potential, otherwise, he was going to be fired.

"I am Natalia. Here in America people don't like to say how old they are, but I have no problems with that. I am fifty years old and have been married for thirty years. Let me tell you that if I were the CEO" – she explained with a strong Russian accent– "I would send many of you to a better training than these tango lessons."

That was Natalia's style; her skinny body and blond hair didn't match her direct, tactless, abrasive, and sincere way of talking. She had to improve her communication skills and listen better, otherwise she would never succeed in the company.

The room was getting hotter because of the lack of air conditioning. Kashi was slowly getting upset and blaming the company for not providing a better, cooler, place for the lessons. She had been born with a leg a half-inch shorter than the other, and from a very young age she learned to blame others for her disgraces. Her sharp mind had brought her success wherever she worked, but sooner or later her "blame others" attitude had prevented her from moving forward professionally.

"I am Kashi, like my mom and my grandmother and many more of my ancestors. In India we are a family of many generations that can be traced back many centuries. I look forward to learn something from this training, but if I don't, I am sure it's because my legs. You know, I was born with one leg shorter than the other. Besides, this room is so hot that I can't imagine anybody learning to dance here without getting very tired after the first two minutes."

Carlos reached the thermostat behind him and set it to a lower temperature and said: "Well, the excuse of the air conditioning is fixed. The short leg problem is not really a big problem; my wife used to have one short leg too, but was my dance partner for many, many years."

He quickly realized that Kashi was complaining even before the lesson started, so he lied about his wife having a shorter leg to dismiss her argument. Virginia, who was next, was smiling because she knew that Kashi always blamed others and took no responsibility for her mistakes. Virginia had a different problem; even though she was clever and hardworking, she always saw herself less than capable to do the job. Her self-esteem and self-confidence were low.

"Hi, I am Virginia. My family comes from Florence, Italy, but I was born in Michigan, lived there all my life, and two years ago I found this job in New York. I have never tried any kind of embraced dancing, and I think it's going to be hard for me to learn it. I feel intimidated. I really can't see myself as a tango dancer."

Carlos had seen all kind of students in his fifty years of teaching, so he immediately recognized her lack of confidence and knew what to say to her.

"Virginia, could you step forward for me?"

And after she did, he immediately said, "You have just given the first tango step, and it was a very beautiful one. What are you so afraid of? The fastest way to learn is by making mistakes."

She didn't understand what he was talking about, but for some reason she felt good after his compliment. She smiled and went back to the line.

The last in the circle of students was C.Y., a short thin man of Asian complexion, with a grave voice and very sharp mind. He had been first in his graduating class, more than 40 years ago. His wife had left him for a much younger guy few months ago, leaving him emotionally devastated. Many in the company thought he was going to be the next CEO before John M. Crawford was appointed by the board last month. A couple of mistakes he had made during the time he was dealing with his wife's departure cost him the CEO position. He had never been good at handling details and learning from his few mistakes, and that had worsened when he was left alone at home.

"Hello Carlos. I am C.Y.. I've been in this company for 30 years, more than anybody in this room. At my age I can hardly believe I could learn to dance tango, but I'll give it my best."

"Thank you all for your introductions, guys. You all will learn to tango. I promise you. Let me tell you this: you are who *you* believe you are. In order to become a good tango dancer you first must believe you will become one. If you don't believe in yourself, nobody else will, and you will have hard times achieving your goals. If you believe you are a good financial advisor, you have fulfilled the minimum requirement to be one."

"As you already know, I am Carlos, your tango instructor"– he said with a strong Argentine accent. "I have been teaching tango for decades, many decades, and I have given lessons to Hollywood and Broadway dancers, as well as to other CEOs whose names I can't disclose because they don't want other people to know. I am young. This is how I feel, and how you feel is more important than your calendar age. I have been single for about ten years, since my wife passed away. So, if you know any single woman who is as young as I am, please don't hesitate to introduce me to her."

Lessons were to be five full days of learning intense tango techniques that would, hopefully, transform them forever as dancers and, more importantly for the company, as successful leaders. Students knew each other well, their weaknesses and strengths, but only as coworkers. The boot camp was going to be the first time they would share so many hours together, in a different environment, learning something for the first time, all of them at the same time. It was going to be an opportunity for the fast learners of the team.

Carlos was an old school Argentine tango instructor with a lot of character and a sharp wit. Raised in the oldest neighborhood of Buenos Aires, San Telmo, he had learned the art of tango at the age of ten, while dancing with older fellow dancers. That was common in Buenos Aires, older male dancers practiced their steps and moves with younger boys of the same weight and height as the women with whom they wanted to dance. It benefited both parties: boys learned the woman's steps, and the men practiced their own.

"In this tango I will teach you," Carlos said, "the main goal is to dance like one entity. It is not a man and a woman dancing together, but an entity made of a man and a woman that moves on the floor as one, at unison with the beat of the tango music. Both are leading the steps and both are following the steps. Compare it to a pair of professional ice skaters. When you are watching them on the floor, do you see the man or the woman leading? or following? No! They are a single person moving smoothly on the ice. That is what happens in tango. There are no leaders and no followers, only a man and a woman dancing on the wooden floor. However, and this is the difficulty in learning tango, one of the dancers must initiate the movement. One of the two has to invite the other to perform a specific step. By tradition, the person who has taken that role of the inviter has been the man, while the woman, almost instantaneously, accepting the invitation, follows the step in unison. A good tango dancer who plays the role of the woman usually follows the lead, or invitation, seamlessly from the man that plays the role of the leader. There are occasions when the woman role is that of initiating the steps, and on those occasions, it is the man's responsibility to follow her and make the step to look and feel unified."

That long comment was enough for Miranda to get upset. A woman from New York couldn't accept she had to follow a man just because she was a woman. She almost quit the lesson when she heard that. "If I am going to be learning how to follow orders from these guys" —Miranda said as she finger-pointed her male colleagues— "then I quit."

"Don't worry," said Carlos calmly. "Let me continue my explanation before you make a bad decision. Leading and following are two extremes of the same continuum. Every one of us in this room was born with a degree of leadership and a degree of follower-ship. Nobody is a pure leader or a pure follower. So, to be a *tanguero* or a *tanguera*, you must learn the steps of the man as well as the steps of a woman. You cannot be a leader if you don't know how to follow, and vice-verse. Think in this way: the best follower is always the leader. The leader believes in his or her own ideas one hundred percent and follows them fully committed. That means, the leader is the best follower! So, the distinction between a leader and a follower is simply for convenience during my lessons, but in reality, they are both the same concept at different levels of a continuum. From now on, just to simplify things, I will not use the words man's role or woman's role, but rather I will use leader and follower, and some times, inviter and invitee."

Miranda calmed down and stayed quiet. Carlos waited for her response, but she evaded his gaze. Camila, who hadn't taken her beautiful eyes off Carlos form the very beginning, raised her hand and asked Carlos what tango meant for him.

Carlos, who still had the stamina of a young man, observed Camila, from head to toe, not hiding his admiration of her beauty. Then he said:

"Tango is a passionate, sensual, and non-verbal communication between a man and a woman with tango music in the background. That is all. You'll have to learn to communicate effectively under those terms, here on the dancing floor. Now, listen carefully, whenever there is a man and a woman communicating with each other, that's the seed of society, the seed of a family, the seed of life itself. Therefore, tango is a re-flexion of life. Whatever happens in the dance floor also happens in life. A man and a woman talking on the street is the same as a man and a woman dancing tango on this wooden floor."

Students were slowly realizing why they had been sent to take lesson with Carlos. Each sentence he dropped mirrored what teachers in business schools had told them years ago.

"Well, let's start with today's lesson" —Carlos said. "I'll request from you one thing only: to be fully present. Focus your attention to my teachings; don't wander mentally. Being focused is the key to success on anything you do in life. The mind has almost infinite power if you focus its attention to a single subject. If you go astray in your thoughts, you dilute your mind's ability to learn quickly and well."

The Stance

The first lesson was about the tango stance, one of the most important characteristics of a good tango dancer. Carlos went around the room checking the posture of each student. The chest had to be forward, the chin up, knees slightly bent, the balance stable. He made sure that the body weight was under the ball of their feet, but still with a vertical and extended spine, without wobbling sideways or tipping over.

"Show your forward intention, your confidence, even when you are standing still," he said. "Never retreat before you start, keep your own balance no matter what your partner is doing, and maintain flexibility to improve your balance and to be ready for sudden changes in the music. Always stay balanced yourself. Don't lean on your partner because she or he will become tired and you won't be working as a team, in unison."

Each one of his sentences was a concise, clear and short metaphor that applied to tango and to many other things in life. He never repeated them, but he showed many times how to stand, how to be a tango dancer, in the man's role, in the women's role, as a leader or as a follower.

"Any questions?" He asked.

All ten students were intimidated by the authoritative figure of this five-foot tall old man. Nobody said anything. He smiled to relax them, while showing them how to stand in the *tango way.* Then he put his arms in position, as if he were embracing a woman. He then asked them to do the same, and observed them.

"What happened? Did you feel anything?" He asked. He always asked questions. That is a trademark of a leader. Those who ask, are in control of the flow of ideas. C.Y., who kept wobbling each time he tried to be still, answered by saying that he didn't feel anything, and that he didn't understand the purpose of the exercise. That was the answer Carlos had been waiting for.

"Good comment," Carlos said. "You see, C.Y., I can tell that you aren't a man who pays attention to the details. You are a man of vision and big ideas. That is good for a leader, but at the same time, you have to pay attention to the minute things happening around you, in the dance floor, or in your life. Tango will teach you that. You listen to your partner, feel his or her weight transferring from one foot to the other. You have to be aware of your body's own axis. This is at the core of your values; be aware of your own balance and of the changes you experience because of your movements and decisions. Always be aware of the environment and yourself. Anybody can take the large steps -- that's easy -- but the fine and careful movements, my friend, those are the difficult ones. Don't shy away from details because they give us the flavor of life. Actually, C.Y., if you practice the role of the woman while you learn tango, you will develop that awareness for details much quicker. Try it."

C.Y. was perplexed about how Carlos had already seen one of his main problems as a professional. Lack of attention to details had been brought up in job performance evaluations his entire life. In his first attempt to learn the details of tango dancing, he closed his eyes, set his arm in embracing position, and listened to his body, carefully. He focused his mind to *read* his body, and then he felt it: a slight pressure in the ball of his standing foot, and the muscles in his back compensating the unbalanced weight of his arms. "This is it," he said to himself, "I think I know what he is talking about."

After several minutes, Carlos asked them to shift weight to the other foot and extend backward their left foot. They had to keep that position for more than five minutes, with their arms in embracing position. A few minutes later they had no strength left in their bodies.

"Can we have a break?" Asked Kashi; always complaining.

"We are just warming up, Kashi," Carlos replied. "Keep working; don't be lazy. In tango, the energy you put in, is energy you take out later on. It's like physics."

After a couple of more minutes Carlos gave them permission to rest:

"Good enough. You may rest now. But remember, practice puts you closer to perfection. The harder you work, the more fruit you will harvest at the end of the day. Practice until the movement feels natural, effortless. Practice until your body moves in the *tango way* without you being aware of it."

After five minutes, they resumed the exercise and repeated it several times for several hours, until each student was completely exhausted, but fully in control of their balance and aware of the changes produced by the movement of their arms.

"Very well. Take a break. Working isn't everything in life." Carlos said with a smile.

Kashi approached him to complain. She was wearing a beautiful white silk coat and several gold rings in her fingers. She explained, again, that she had a short leg and she couldn't keep her balance. Carlos was an old-school teacher, a sort of drill sergeant, and didn't like her attitude. He knew that a short leg was not an impediment to balance.

"Kashi, you can't blame external factors for your own limitations or mistakes. You have to take responsibilities for your actions, always. If by any chance your physical limitations don't let you be the best dancer or whatever, then you have to fight back, and if you can't fight back, then you may settle for the second best. But if you complain even before you start, then you are not going to get ahead. For instance, if I lead a bad step, or if I step on my follower's feet, or if I hesitate in my step invitations, then I acknowledge it, take responsibility, and move on. I don't go around saying that my partner is in fault. When you learn to take responsibilities for your actions, you'll see how much more you can do."

Kashi didn't reply and turned around, infuriated, but recognized he was right. Augusto, who had been listening to the conversation between Carlos and Kashi, wanted to say something to the instructor; he wanted to defend Kashi, who was his next door office partner.

However, as always, Augusto hesitated. He didn't have the guts to confront Carlos. His lack of determination had very often prevented him from doing the right thing at the right time. But the old guy was too experienced. He realized Augusto was uncomfortable with the situation by just looking at his body language; that was a skill Carlos had learned from the tango embrace.

"Did you want to say anything, Augusto?" Asked Carlos. "Don't be afraid of taking the first step, be confident and determine. Believe in your guts and your principles. Just say it."

Augusto felt challenged by the instructor, and that prompted him to say what he was holding back.

"Yes, I want to tell you something," he replied. "I don't know how to say it, but I think you are being too tough on Kashi. She has a physical handicap and you want her to ignore it. That is not fair."

Carlos kept a square face, immutable and defiant, but after a moment, he smiled. He smiled because he knew Augusto was changing, changing for the better.

"Well said, Augusto," he said. "Let's ask Kashi directly. What do you think, Kashi?"

She was still surprised seeing Augusto speaking up to defend her. She ignored Carlos' question, and facing Augusto, she said,

"Thank you, Augusto. I didn't know you were so courageous. I know myself, and also know I have to stop blaming others, but thank you for standing up for me."

And she walked away. Carlos, always confident, smiled again, because he had accomplished his goal. Kashi recognized she had to change, and Augusto had learned to speak up, and to take the first step before it was too late.

The Walk

Each kind of dance has its own steps, but in tango, steps are not as important as the walk. Better said, if there is no tango walk, steps won't make your dance look like tango. It takes years to develop the tango walk, but once learned, steps come easily. Carlos began walking around the room, close to the walls, always with the walls on his right. After several minutes without saying a word, he stopped and asked them what was the difference between a regular walk and the tango walk? Students were quiet. They saw a difference, but didn't know how to describe it.

"The tango walk has a purpose," Carlos answered himself. "It has an intention, a determination, a force and energy that propel you with gusto and passion, but at the same time it is smooth, tender, silent, stealthy, as if you were sliding on a polished wooden floor covered with silk. This is difficult for the leader, because finding the right balance between force and softness requires much practice. And for the same reasons, it is difficult for the follower who should present resistance to the leader's force, but still has to follow the leader while preserving independence and balance."

That was the essence of the tango walk. Chest should be forward, even when walking backwards. The head should not bounce vertically. The feet skim the floor, but do not make noise. Shoes should brush each other when legs pass next to the other. Each step is completed only when the imaginary axis that goes through your head - neck - chest - guts is also aligned with the supporting foot, balanced and steady.

Miranda, who always wanted to do things with the minimal effort, asked how fast should the steps be.

"In tango," Carlos replied, "when you walk, you can go as slow or as fast as you want, as long as the couple is following to the beat of the tango song. But one thing is very important: never ever stop moving! Inaction doesn't belong here, nor in your work, your family, your life. Inaction kills you silently. It kills relationships, ideas, prosperity, and everything else. How can you achieve your goals and success in life if you stop moving? So, keep always doing something," he said while still walking around the room. "Even when you pause, you are moving. You follow the movement of your breath, as well as the resulting breath of your partner."

He kept walking until all students realized that they had to follow him; they followed the leader by imitating his actions, not his words. There was no music, just the floor, the walls, and the walk. They walked until it was time for the lunch break.

"Go and have a good lunch," Carlos told them. "Resting and eating are complementary to work. Never let work interfere with your healthy habits."

Camila waited until all were out of the room, and approached Carlos with a smile.

"Hi. I have a question. Do you know what kind of shoes should I buy for tango?"

He smiled, knowing that she didn't wait to be alone with him just to ask about shoes. He replied with the usual recommendations. "Buy two pairs, one for the lessons and another for the parties. Make sure they have good support of your heels, and that they are not so tall that you can't be on the ball of your feet. Other than that, pick the style you like. Beige should go well with your beautiful skin tone."

"Thank you. I didn't know I had to buy two pairs," she said.

A silence filled the empty room with the maple wooden floor, and they both watched each other in the mirror that covered the entire wall of the room. He waited for her to ask a real question, and she waited for him to ask her to go out for lunch. He smiled and threw the hook: "Well, I guess I have to go for lunch."

"Why don't we go together to a café across the street?" She said even before he finished talking.

He smiled again and agreed.

The Music

Tango came into existence in the 1880's, when Argentines and Uruguayans created it. It is a music without drums, but with a strong, easily recognizable beat. Old tangos were played with guitars and flutes, but they have evolved to a point where any instrument can be used to play it. However, the most distinctive and prominent tango instrument is the *bandoneón*, a modified accordion of German origin that was introduced to Argentina in the early 1900's. A tango without a *bandoneón* lacks authenticity and force.

Carlos entered the room with a big smile. In one hand he carried a *bandoneón* case, and in the other, a laptop case. It was an interesting image of two artifacts separated by about a century, coexisting harmoniously in the arms of this traditional *tanguero*. He opened the *bandoneón* and explained a little history of the instrument. Then he opened his laptop and played one of the most famous tangos, *El Choclo*.

"The music is the thread of the conversation," he said and waited for the student's reaction. Virginia, who kept saying to herself she couldn't learn tango, asked what conversation he was talking about.

"Great question!" Carlos said. "Everything in life is a conversation. It may be between a man and a woman; between a child and a mother; even between things that don't talk, like a pencil and a hand, or a paper and a pencil. Every conversation has a theme, a thread. In tango, the music is the most important part of the conversation between the dancing partners. For any couple, dancers or not, they have to find the right music that allows them to communicate fluidly, that fills in for the lack of words and makes the conversation seamless. Tango is a wordless conversation between the two dancers. Each dancer understands what the other says – without words – because they are both listening to the same melody, the same lyrics, the same beat, and the wordless moves of our bodies in contact. Words are replaced by the physical touch of our bodies, the movement of our shoulders, the pressure in our hands, the smell, the warmth of our chests; all that is part of the conversation."

"That is too abstract," replied Virginia, while combing with her fingers her black long hair that reached her waist.

Carlos smiled again, paused for a moment, thinking how to reply. Meanwhile, Wilmer was impatient, waiting for the class to start. He needed to work; he needed to be doing something. His hands were itching.

"Why don't we start the class?" Wilmer burped, and then smiled.

"Work and more work," said Carlos. "That's what you want, don't you, Wilmer? You wait for instructions, but don't take the initiative. For example, help me answer Virginia's questions. She said that the conversation in tango was an abstract concept. What do you say to that?"

A good leader knows how to use his resources, and Carlos was a maestro doing that. Besides, he had put Wilmer in the spotlight, forcing him to be creative in his response.

"Give me an analogy that explains the conversation in tango," Carlos insisted. Wilmer was struggling to come up with something out of the box; his many years of routine and obedient work had left him lacking ideas. He went deep to his thoughts and suddenly said something.

"Well," Wilmer replied, "I think that what you are trying to say is that the music of tango serves as the common theme of a conversation that help us, the dancing partners, to dance as one. The conversation is simply the give and take between me and her, until we synchronously dance as if we knew each other for years. That is what I call a well-oiled machine. When I engage with my clients, when I read their concerns, we communicate and work much better."

That was an amazing answer from a person that had to improvise on the spot. Manuel, the CEO, knew what he was doing by choosing him for this class.

"That was a truly excellent response, Wilmer," Carlos replied. "We could call that *empathy* with your client." I want each of you to develop that empathy with your partner. That is part of being a good listener, a good tango dancer. He then turned his face to Virginia looking for a nod of understanding. She smiled.

"A tango dancer," he continued, "must make sure that the partner is synchronized, and the best way to do that is by both following the same tune. It is the tune that keeps the conversation of our bodies fluid without hiccups, and our dance as precise and perfect as it can be."

They listened to El Choclo several times, until they could identify the melodic and the rhythmic passages of the song. Carlos asked them to start walking to the rhythm. After hearing the song so many times, they were able to adapt their steps to the slow and fast passages and maintain smoothness while walking. Virginia went to say something she had never said before. "This seems easy to me. I think I can learn this."

Carlos heard that, and quickly replied. "Great, Virginia, great. Whatever you think you can do, you will do. Everything starts from inside yourself. That is more powerful than reacting to some external input. If you generate your own energy, then you are on the path towards achieving your goals. If you just react, then your success will depend on the external input, which you may not control."

Carlos was very satisfied with the responses from his students, especially from Virginia and Wilmer who had taken a big step forward in the improvement of their character. Students kept walking for several hours until El Choclo drove them crazy. Carlos called for the end of the lesson; it was time to rest and they all left, except for Camila who had stayed behind to wait for Carlos, again.

The Embrace

There they were in their fourth lesson and Carlos had not made them dance together yet. It's hard to learn any dance if you don't interact with your partner, but that was the method Carlos had developed over the many years of teaching. He entered the room looked each student at their eyes and said:

"A good posture and a good tango walk without a good embrace is like having a good recipe and the perfect ingredients but never cooking the meal. A good tango dancer has to have a good embrace, a solid, respectful engagement with the dancing partner. In your jargon, the embrace is a three minute long handshake with your future business partner. Now, watch me."

And he asked Camila to come forward. He embraced her, surrounding her body with his right arm, softly, tenderly, and fully, feeling the heat of her core. Just for a few seconds, he swung in place and then released the embrace. She smiled with shyness, enjoying the feeling of heat that runs from the stomach to the head like bubbles in a soda drink. The men were unaware of what had just happened, but the women were mesmerized, observing Camila's reaction. None had danced with Carlos until that day. He asked Camila what she had felt, and she said she couldn't describe it, but it was "special;" she also said she felt taken care of. As soon as she said that, all men turned their attention on her, and started to watch more carefully. Carlos smiled.

"A good embrace allows your partner to feel taken cared of, and in doing so, building trust. If two partners distrust each other, how can they cooperate? How can they dance in unison. But be sure the embrace is reciprocal, not just one-sided. I cannot dance with a dead person; I need energy from my partner. I need a hug, a tango hug that says *I am alive and want to embrace you too.* If my partner is non-responsive, it is like kissing a dead person. I don't trust someone that doesn't want to engage with me at the same level I want."

Effectively, trust development is the first requirement for a tango dancer, or better said, for any person that looks for success and leadership of any kind. If the partner does not trust you he or she will never be committed to the cause. By embracing a stranger of the opposite gender with such proximity, chest-to-chest, cheek-to-cheek, you are trusting him or her with your private space, and once that trust is built, the dance becomes easier for both. If one of the dancers is too shy to share that private space, he or she will have difficulties learning how to tango. Conversely, if one of the dancers is too aggressive in the dance, he or she must become less so as to allow the partner to gain the trust they need to dance better. In summary, tango takes away the shyness and aggression of people to put them in the middle of the spectrum, and once there, slowly, they build the trust for each other.

"Please embrace the person you have on your right," Carlos asked.

Jerome laughed out loud when he heard that. He said he couldn't dance with the person to his right because it was a man too. Besides, C.Y. was a short man who barely reached Jerome's chest.

"If you want to be successful, you don't discriminate based on gender!" said Carlos with stern face. "Do you do business with women only?"

Jerome didn't know what to say. His smile disappeared immediately. He turned to his right, and embraced C.Y., who not quite convinced either, accepted the embrace. They didn't know for what kind of embrace Carlos was asking. So, they hugged for two seconds and separated. Carlos observed and smiled.

"Jerome, what is the goal of this exercise?" Carlos asked.

"I don't know," he replied.

"Remember this for the rest of your life, Jerome." – Carlos continued – "Don't obey any instruction if you don't know the purpose, the goal and the motivation behind it. You've got to think, you've got to layout your goals and work toward them. If you don't have your own dreams and goals, if you just follow commands from others, your success will never be yours, but theirs. Got it? Now, you have to hug the same way you would hug your brother after not seeing him for years. I want to see a real hug. Watch me again."

This time, Carlos asked Raymond to embrace him. Raymond did it the best he could, but Carlos still looked disappointed. Raymond was very disturbed embracing an old macho guy that, according to Raymond, lacked sensitivity towards the students. Raymond was more interested in the interacting with his work partners, as well as in the multiple phone calls and text messages he kept receiving while in the lessons. That had been slowly infuriating Carlos.

"If the embrace is not comfortable," Carlos said, "if your partner doesn't feel a connection, if you treat your partner like a mop that can be shuffled from left to right without care, then your partner will quit and leave you alone at the first opportunity."

Raymond's phone rang one more time, and Carlos had to say something. Carlos had been trying to ignore the calls, but he couldn't anymore.

"The day that you focus all your energy in one thing, and only one thing, that is the day you will make the first step in the direction of your goals," Carlos said, glaring at Raymond. "For three days I have been ignoring your distractions, but I cannot take it anymore. Please turn off the damn phone, put your attention on what I say and do, and learn the skills of focus and concentration."

Raymond seemed perplexed by Carlos' mandatory tone. He turned off his phone, and sat down. He didn't dance for the rest of the lesson, but never took his eyes from Carlos' instructions until the end of the day.

Carlos decided to embrace each student, one by one, until they learned how to embrace in the tango way: with care, with passion, with acknowledgement, with reciprocity. All those things are needed to engage with a partner, either on the dance floor or outside it.

"Now embrace your partner again, walk, and listen," Carlos asked.

"Remember," he continued, "we are talking with our bodies, not with words. So, listen to your partner; listen to the moves of the chest, the warmth of the hand, the sweat of the face, the smell of the perfume, and above all, listen to the feet through the movement of the chest. You have to develop your hypersensitivity to perfect the art of dancing tango."

Camila, seeing that Raymond was sitting down, realized she had no partner to practice the embrace, so she insisted in practicing with Carlos. While doing that, she murmured to his ears: "I think I learned how to do this already. I want to go to the next level." Carlos understood what she meant by "next level," but preferred to use the opportunity to give her one more lesson on character. He replied, also murmuring to her ears, "I think you don't know what you think you know. The moment you say *I learned it*, you close the opportunity to learn more, to grow more, to develop a deeper understanding of the matter. You are just learning how to embrace, but you are not listening to my body. You have to keep learning, in this class and for the rest of your life."

Camila didn't like his lecturing attitude, but replied to his words with: "I wasn't taking about tango."

To which he replied quickly: "I know, but that other subject doesn't belong to this lesson. The other nine students deserve my full attention. Honesty and responsibility towards them come before our relationship."

That answer was clear as water for Camila. She never broached the subject again during lessons. In the mean time, the rest of students were stumbling in their walk, stepping on toes, hitting knees, losing their balance, and couldn't advance more than two steps without having at least one of these problems.

"Stop," said Carlos. "You see what happened? Walking alone is easy, but walking and embracing someone at the same time is a different story. Living single all your life is easy, but living married is much more difficult. In tango, the inviter has to make sure that his instructions are clear, unambiguous, with a goal in mind. The invitee can then read the invitation and follow. It is a communication in both directions, if the invitee is consistent, the inviter can improve his skills, and the better the invitations are, the more consistent the invitee will be."

All dancers kept working on their walk and embrace and soon they began feeling more confident and stable. Few good instructions gave them the ability to be better tango dancers. Carlos went around checking each couple and giving suggestions, individually and as a couple. Augusto and Miranda had definitely and finally connected, since they had maintained a close, very close, embrace for long periods of time, and seemed to enjoy each other very much.

Carlos then turned on the music – El Choclo again – and the dancers got even better.

"Do you see how much easier is to dance with the music on?" Carlos asked. "The tango is the thread of the conversation, remember? You both have to have an ear for the music and another ear for the chest of your partner. Don't send bad signals with your chest. If the direction of any step is unclear, your partner will get confused. Listen men, your chest should move in one, and only one direction. If you hesitate, if you don't know where you are going, your partner will know even less so. Listen women, your chest should also move is one direction, in unison with your partner. If you try to anticipate the step, you may guess sometimes, but at other times you will go in different direction, or at a different pace. Also remember to keep your ankles soft; neither partner should feel the foot of the other partner hitting the floor. Be soft spoken with your feet."

Natalia, who was dancing with Wilmer and had been quiet all lesson long, burst with anger, "I can't hear anything from his chest. I quit."

"Nobody quits here!" shouted Carlos. "If you want to succeed at something, you persevere; you keep trying; you make mistakes and learn from them, but you don't quit."

He was angry too. He detested quitters. His dad had left the family home when he was only five years old, and since then had learned that those who quit leave many wounded behind.

Natalia realized she had spoken too bluntly, as always. She rephrased it the best she could: "Excuse me, Carlos, I didn't mean to upset you. What I meant to say was that listening to the music and to Wilmer's chest at the same time is hard to do."

Carlos also realized his words had been too harsh to her. He approached her and asked her to dance together to practice the embrace and the tango walk. She was so skinny that he could wrap around her completely with his arm. They danced for several minutes, with him correcting her at every needed situation. She learned to listen and ended up with a better embrace, better posture and better walk as well.

"Wow, dancing with you makes a big difference," she said while waving her hand next to her neck to get some fresh air. "It's hot in here. Man, how do you do that?"

She blushed like a tomato and gained composure after a few minutes. She took a deep breath to calm herself. She got aroused too easily. Not a surprise since her husband of thirty years left her five years ago, and she hadn't had any kind of intimacy since then.

"You really know how to talk with your chest," she continued, trying to elicit a comment from Carlos.

"Yes, that is the goal," said Carlos. "Each of you has to learn how to communicate better, more clearly, more effectively, using the tools made available to you.

In the tango, your embrace is the main channel of communication between you and your partner. In life, you can talk; you can gesture; you can cry; you can sing, and you can even have sex; you have many more ways to express your ideas and feelings; but in tango, all you can do is to embrace your partner and let him or her know what you are feeling and thinking with the minute moves of the muscles of your body."

Natalia listened with attention and realized she had a long way to go before reaching the level of subtle communication skills needed for her to master tango.

All of the students danced for hours, with few breaks for water and rest. Carlos kept correcting them, one by one, until they understood the role of the leader and of the follower. He then asked them to switch roles. He insisted on the idea that a successful tango dancer needs to understand both sides of the story. If one doesn't develop empathy, then working in unison becomes very difficult. Remember, leadership and follower-ship are extremes of the same continuum.

The Two Paradoxes

Walking around the room Carlos approached each student and pushed them, one by one, separately. They were puzzled but having fun with the exercise. And then he asked:

"We know that in tango one partner is responsible for navigating the floor. That is the inviter, usually the man. Meanwhile, the invitee trusts the inviter and follows the lead that results in the steps. It is usually the female dancer who plays this role in tango. It means that most of the time, the man is walking forward and the woman is walking backwards, into a direction where she cannot see. My question is: does a woman's energy and force move forward or backward while she walks?"

Simplistically thinking it seems that since the woman is walking backward, she has an energy and force that also go backward, but if we think a bit more, it is clear that the woman has to produce a force forward as well. If the inviter is pushing and the invitee were pulling, they would be running and accelerating all the time.

"There is nothing more destructive than a complacent follower," Carlos said. "Someone that never refutes, never debates, never questions destroys the engagement, the embrace. A person dancing as invitee, as a follower, has to find the right balance between pushing forward and walking backwards. A leader that encounters no resistance eventually becomes a tyrant in the dance floor. The same happens in life. The president of a country with a bunch of adoring followers will end up doing whatever he wants all the time. This is why we need a strong opposition to balance the forces of power. I know this from my own experiences during the dictatorships of Argentina."

He couldn't be more certain. Tango leaders are often at their best when a follower resists, forcing the leader to think of other ways to go, other avenues, other alternatives and improvisations that fuel innovation and add spice to the dance.

"When I went around pushing each one of you, I was testing your skill as a follower," Carlos said. "The follower trains the leader, and vice verse. The more obedient a follower is, the less the leader learns to lead."

That was the first tango paradox, the follower paradox. Being a follower requires you to resist the leader's lead, up to certain point.

"How does a leader know or feel whether a follower is following or leading?" Carlos asked again.

Nobody said anything. That question was the flip side of the coin of the previous question. Good leaders know when things are not working out and revise their position and methods to maintain the engagement of the followers. In essence, good leaders are also followers. They follow their followers. They create new steps, new resolutions; they generate new ideas.

"If the leader loses balance, it is likely that his or her lead made the follower go in a wrong direction. It is the leader's responsibility to change direction to temporarily follow the follower and then return back to the leader's course," Carlos said.

"That is a very difficult thing to learn," Camila said.

"Indeed it is, but that is the beauty of tango, like life, you never stop learning."

That was the leader's paradox. Being the inviter you have to be prepared for the follower's invitations for change, in such a way that the final course of navigation is aligned with the ideas of the person who is playing the role of the leader in the dance. The leader is able to avoid bigger mistakes by following the follower during those moments of unbalance. Followers, on the other hands, feel empowered when they see that their own steps are acknowledged, and their mistakes are compensated. That is part of building trust between the inviter and the invitee.

The Milonga

"What is a milonga?" Carlos asked to start the new lesson.

For many students, it was the first time they had heard that word. Carlos decided it was better if he explained the term.

"Milonga has two meanings; it is the name of a type of tango, and it also is the social dance party where we go to dance tango. The milonga party is the place where you show to your partner what you have learned and you share with him or her that special tango embrace that makes tango such a special dance. Milonga is the place where *tangueros* gather to share and enjoy the company of people with a shared appreciation of the tango music."

We spend most of our life in activities of preparation. Tango is not the exception. Hours and hours of preparation must be spent before going to the dancing floor where dancers follow the tango etiquette and show to their partner what they know. What happens in a milonga is simply the reflection of what happens in a respectful relationship between a man and a woman in real life.

"Why do you think I have played *El Choclo*, and no other song, over and over all these days?" Carlos asked.

Kashi sighed, showing her frustration for listening the same song so many times. "I have been wondering about that," she said out loud and sarcastically.

"Because you like it," said Raymond jokingly.

Carlos waited for an intelligent answer, but nobody seemed in the mood for that. He then said: "Because the more prepared we are, the better our chances to perform well. As in real life, my friends, if you repeat and repeat what you have to do, it becomes an integral part of you."

"But if we go to a milonga we will only know one song, El Choclo!" complains Kashi, while many nodded.

Carlos, smiling, patiently told her not to despair because a single well danced tango was worth more than ten lousily danced ones. Then he sat and asked them to sit too. He wanted to explain the rules of engagement on the tango floor.

"It is important that you learn the basic rules of etiquette in the dancing floor. Going to a milonga is like going to a night club full of people. There are some rules you follow to be accepted in the bar. The same happens at the milonga. First, be honest and fair with everybody you dance with. Don't take advantage of any of them; they will reflect that feeling and treatment back to you. It's human nature. Your partner is your partner, not your enemy. If you enter the relationship with animosity, aggression, or egotism, both sides lose."

"Second," Carlos continued, "when you make a mistake, which should be few if you practice, take responsibility for it and apologize to your partner. Nothing is more annoying than a person who ignores his or her mistakes. But once your apologies are acknowledged, move to the next step, learn and improve from the mistake. Remember that the milonga won't stop because you make a mistake. The same happens outside tango. Life doesn't stop because of your mistake; it continues with or without you."

"Third, be polite. This will serve you in two ways. It will always leave a good impression of you, which will open the door for the next time you ask for another dance. Also, being polite is the best weapon in a dispute. The one that loses control, that becomes violent or aggressive, usually loses the battle, if there is any."

These three rules of etiquette were very simple and concrete. Put in practice, they would benefit each of Carlos' students both in the milonga and in their business.

"In a milonga," he continued, "it is the woman's prerogative to accept an invitation to go to the dancing floor. If she doesn't want to, the inviter or leader, cannot force the dance; again, this is the same as in real life. Of course, there are many ways the invitee can call the attention of a dancing partner. They are, again, very similar to the techniques used in the daily life outside the milonga floor. So, when you enter in a milonga, use your common sense and you will be fine."

Milongas are the fun part of tango. All your hours of training are on display at that time. Many people are drawn to the milonga for the same reasons people go to a social event: to find a partner or to spend time with friends. If there is any mutual attraction, that goes beyond the dancing floor; it is a story that transcends tango and fall in the realm of your personal life.

The Coda

Finally, after five intensive and long days of tango training, it was time for the last lesson. Carlos had invited the students to a different venue, in a nearby building, in a room not much bigger than the old room. When he entered the room, all students, without being instructed, stood up, held their chest high and picked their chin up. The circle of learning had been completed, and the most important lesson was already part of their character: show confidence whenever you act, and success will visit you.

"Thank you. You may sit now," Carlos said. "This lesson is yours. I am not going to teach you any new steps today. You can ask any question and I will try to answer it. In other words, you lead, and I follow."

Kashi, always impatient, asked him how they were supposed to learn tango in one week if he had spent decades learning it?

"Learning is a life commitment, Kashi," he replied. "If you stop learning, you will be mentally dead in a few years. Besides, you will be left behind by your peers because your skill will be obsolete and your chances to advance in your endeavors will diminish. So, you must keep exploring tango your entire life. That is what I have done, and what I am planning to do always."

That was not about tango only, but about every aspect of their lives. Learning becomes the constant in everything we do. Kashi, acknowledged his teaching with a big smile, and knowing this was the last lesson, approached him, hugged him, and gave him a present.

Augusto raised a hand and asked: "I've been watching videos of tango dancers and see them doing more difficult steps than those you taught us here. How can we expect to be good dancer with the few steps you have taught us?"

"What I have taught you are the fundamentals of tango, the building blocks to create your own dance. It is as though I taught you words and grammar, then you go out in life using your intelligence and creativity to learn the language of tango -- you can apply that knowledge to your problems. With these building blocks you can improvise. Your creativity will allow you to create new steps, new things that you and your partner will enjoy in the short journey of one song."

"I also watched some videos with dancers in open embrace. Which form is better, open or close embrace?" asked Augusto again.

Carlos smiled and shook his head from side to side, remembering how many times he had answered that question. Augusto used the concept of "open embrace" which Carlos had not used so far. Carlos replied:

"Oh, Augusto. That is a misconception. There is no close or open embrace. There is only one embrace that has elasticity to accommodate different steps. Some steps are better done in close proximity, "the close embrace." Other steps are better done with a larger separation of the bodies, "the open embrace." Experienced dancers are flexible as they accommodate the distance of their bodies to perform each step. Imagine you are speaking with a client, and you present to him an offer with a degree of risk that he doesn't like. Once you see your client's reaction you will probably present a second offer less risky. In other words, you become elastic in your offers. It's the same with the embrace, not always close, not always open, but changing during the song. Eventually, during the dialogue you gain more knowledge about your partner and yourself."

"But in open embrace they can do fancy steps that I can't do in close embrace!" Insisted Augusto.

"Yes, but at the expense of losing or reducing communication channels with your partner. Going back to my example, you can convince your client to take an offer with the highest risk, but it may be detrimental for him. He may not come back to you if the risks turn out to be real. Also, if you occupy half of the floor because you are doing fancy steps in open embrace, your tango friends may not want to see you at the next milonga. Once you accept the tango etiquette of the milonga, and share the floor with your friends, the dance becomes a social experience rather than a personal performance. But don't get me wrong, open embrace has its legitimate role as one way of expressing the art of tango dancing. Imagine two hundreds couples of ice skaters skating socially in a ice ring. You see? Ice skaters need the full ice ring to show their athleticism and performance skills. Such is the case with the so-called open embrace tango."

Wilmer raised his hand and asked one question that sounded very simple. "How did you know you were going to be a tango instructor for life?"

Carlos paused for a few seconds before giving an answer. He smiled, and said: "This question has to do with your goals in life and what we define as success and happiness. That is probably the most difficult aspect of life. How do we know what we will become? How do we know what we are good at in order to exploit it? I approached it in a simple manner. It may sound cliché, but it worked for me. Before you set your goals, before you define success and happiness, before all that, there are your dreams. They are the seed for everything else that comes after. Take your dreams and make them your goals; take your goals, and define success; reach success and you achieve happiness. That is all there is to it. Again, if you are focused in your dreams and goals, you will get there, sooner or later."

"One more thing," he added, "please surround yourself with the right people; people you trust that have a positive attitude toward life. They will have the most influence in your daily decisions and in the outcome of many of your projects. As we say in South America, *tell me who your friends are, and I will tell who you are!*"

Carlos paused for a second, read the body language of his students and waited for a reaction. Natalia had been wiping off her tears since the beginning of the lesson, and said, very softly, uncharacteristic of her: "Carlos, you have been very accurate in identifying our individual problems that are preventing us from achieving our maximum potential. Your words have elevated us to a higher level and I have no words to express my gratitude for that. Thank you."

"Your are welcome Natalia. I have given you the tools for success," Carlos continued, "but I want to make clear that success doesn't mean material wealth, as many of you have been taught to think. If that were the case, it would be a boring quest that depends on only one numeric quantity. Success is defined by your goals, not by money. If your goals are to help others, and you achieve that, then you are successful. If your goals are to travel around world and you achieve that, then you are successful too. Don't fall in the trap of thinking that success is only for those who achieve large sums of money or fame."

Miranda, Kashi and Virginia had been talking the day before about how many things they had learned in the tango lessons and wanted to show some appreciation to Carlos. They gave him a thank you card that said: *Carlos, you gave us the gift of the close embrace, the gift of the tango music, the gift of the self confidence, self esteem and the gift of love. We all want to thank you for all that we learned from you in the last five days.*

Carlos almost cried while reading the card, but instead, he stood up and invited them into an adjoining room. They didn't know what was going to happen. When they opened the door, they found a large crowd of people, waiting for them. It was a surprise. Carlos had arranged for a milonga party for the last lesson. Miranda had tears of joy about to roll on her cheek. C.Y. and Jerome were also very happy with the surprise. The room had tables covered in red silk and a white flower stood at the center of each table. The floor was made of a beautiful dark oak. The lights were dimmed and the DJ turned the music on as they entered the floor. Miranda noticed with awe and gratification that her boss, John M. Crawford, PaxCap's CEO, was DJing the party as acknowledgement and recognition of the effort made by all ten students. Not surprisingly, the first tango he played was El Choclo. What else could it had been?

As they danced their first song in a real milonga, Carlos watched them with gratification. He remembered the first impression he had of each of them: Jerome, an aimless guy who just followed other people's goals; Miranda, the corner-cutter who didn't expend the effort to connect hard work with success; Virginia, with such lack of self-confidence that didn't allow her advance in her career; C.Y., the visionary who saw the big stones but stumbled with the pebbles on the road; Wilmer, the hard worker whose lack of innovation kept him stuck in his chair for life; Kashi, who didn't take responsibility for her mistakes; Raymond, whose lack of focus made him waste energy in poorly executed tasks; Natalia, the rude talker, who struggled to communicate her ideas; Augusto, who was always afraid of taking the first step, but had just asked Miranda to dance once again; and Camila, his favorite student, who thought that all she needed to learn in life she had already learned.

Carlos saw them grow as tango dancers, but more importantly for him, he gave them new tools to forge their new character to become better leaders and more successful human beings.

"That is what tango taught me," Carlos said to himself.

Acknowledgement

I want to acknowledge the help I received from my friends and family members while writing this book. You are too many to fit in one page, but you know who you are. Thank you very much. Special thanks go to Marianna Anderle de Sylor for her great job as editor; to Niel, Katiuska and Isabelle for their feedback on the final version; to my sons Daniel, Diego and my wife Nazaret who always gave me a sincere criticism. To all of you I dedicate this book.

C.A.S.A.
Ann Arbor
Fall 2010

www.ingramcontent.com/pod-product-compliance
Lightning Source LLC
Chambersburg PA
CBHW031328040426
42443CB00005B/260